INSPIRE

KYLE BUSCH

BY MARY BLECKWEHL

AMICUS LEARNING

Inspire is published by
Amicus Learning, an imprint of Amicus
P.O. Box 227
Mankato, MN 56002
www.amicuspublishing.us

Editor: Ana Brauer
Series Designer: Kathleen Petelinsek
Book Designer and Photo Researcher: Emily Dietz

Library of Congress Cataloging-in-Publication Data
Names: Bleckwehl, Mary E., author.
Title: Kyle Busch / by Mary Bleckwehl.
Description: Mankato, MN : Amicus Learning, 2026. | Series: Inspire | Includes bibliographical references and index. | Audience: Ages 5–9 | Audience: Grades 2–3 | Summary: "Learn about NASCAR driver Kyle Busch and his accomplishments in an engaging profile packed with photos and fact-filled text suitable for young readers. Includes table of contents, glossary, further resources, and index" — Provided by publisher.
Identifiers: LCCN 2024044113 (print) | LCCN 2024044114 (ebook) | ISBN 9798892005197 (library binding) | ISBN 9798892005739 (paperback) | ISBN 9798892006279 (ebook)
Subjects: LCSH: Busch, Kyle—Juvenile literature. | NASCAR (Association)—Juvenile literature.
Classification: LCC GV1032.B892 B54 2026 (print) | LCC GV1032.B892 (ebook) | DDC 796.72092—dc23/eng/20241204
LC record available at https://lccn.loc.gov/2024044113
LC ebook record available at https://lccn.loc.gov/2024044114

Photo Credits: Associated Press/Alex Menendez, 13, Austin McAfee/Icon Sportswire, cover, Nigel Kinrade, 16; Getty Images/Al Messerschmidt, 10, Icon Sports Wire, 6, James Gilbert, 17, Jared C. Tilton, 5, Jonathan Ferrey, 14, Robert Laberge, 9, Sean Gardner, 4, 20–21, Sun Sentinel, 18; Shutterstock/Pavlo Lys, 11, Ruth Black, 15; Wikimedia Commons/Champions title belts, 19

Printed in India

Table of Contents

A Racing Champion

The driver in car number 18 loves long races. This one is 267 laps. His car has led for 41 laps. The car zooms to the finish line. Kyle Busch wins the NASCAR Cup Championship! He is one of the best NASCAR drivers ever.

DID YOU KNOW?

Busch drove No. 18, the "M&M" NASCAR car, from 2008 to 2022. Now, he drives No. 8, a Chevrolet Camaro ZL1.

Kyle Busch won the NASCAR Cup Championship in 2015 and 2019.

Busch (#4) races three other Legends cars in 2003.

An Early Start

A go-kart was Busch's first racing car at age six. Busch steered. His dad pushed the gas pedal. He liked helping his dad work on cars. At 13, Busch started racing **Legends** cars. He won 65 Legends races.

Childhood Hero

Busch saw NASCAR star Jeff Gordon win many races. He wanted to be as good as Gordon. Busch's mom said he could race if he got good grades. This **motivated** him to do well in school.

Jeff Gordon is one of the most popular NASCAR drivers of all time.

In 2004, Busch won the Funai 250 race in Richmond, Virginia. This race helped him win Rookie of the Year.

NASCAR Debut

At 16 years old, Busch made his NASCAR **debut** in 2001. He raced in the Truck Series. At 18, he began driving in the NASCAR Xfinity Series. He won Rookie of the Year in 2004!

NICKNAMES
Busch has many nicknames. Rowdy, Wild Thing, the Candy Man, and Shrub are some of them.

A Crash to Remember

In February 2015, Busch's car veered off the Daytona track at 176 mph (283 km/h). It crashed into a concrete wall. The car started on fire. Safety workers lifted him out. He broke his right leg and left foot. Busch wondered if he would race again.

Monster Energy was one of Busch's sponsors during the 2015 Xfinity Series.

Busch races around Victory Lane after winning the 2015 Cup Series championship.

The Comeback Kid

Busch missed racing following his injuries. He worked hard to get better. Three months after his crash, he was back on the track. Six months later, the unexpected happened. Busch won his first NASCAR Cup Series championship!

BIRTHDAY WISH

What does a racer want for their birthday? A win, of course! Busch won a race on two of his birthdays.

Family of Racers

Busch has two kids, Brexton (pictured) and a daughter.

The Busch family has three **generations** of racers. Busch's father was a **short-track** racer. Kyle's brother, Kurt, raced NASCAR tracks for 23 years. His son Brexton, born in 2015, is carrying on the family tradition. Brexton started racing at age five in **box stock** cars.

DID YOU KNOW?

Kyle and Kurt Busch have 96 combined NASCAR wins. That is more than any other brothers in NASCAR history.

Ruoff
VICTORY LANE
GEICO
McLAREN CUSTOM GRILLS
CUP SERIES

Busch greets his fans before a race.

Giving Back

After each race, Busch thanks those who have helped him. His appreciation goes beyond the track. He donated his first Cup Series winnings to help Hurricane Katrina victims. The Kyle Busch Foundation helps children in need. The Kyle's Miles program helps dogs in shelters.

DID YOU KNOW?

Busch is a professional wrestling fan. In 2019, he won a World Wrestling Entertainment (WWE) 24/7 Championship.

Racing Ahead

Kyle Busch still has his foot on the gas! He races in all three of the NASCAR national series, the Cup, Xfinity, and Truck. In 2023, he won three Cup Series races. He hopes to one day race alongside his son. Until then, his plan is to keep winning!

In 2023, Busch won the GEICO 500 race at Talladega Superspeedway in Alabama.

SUPER STATS

KYLE THOMAS BUSCH

Birthday: May 2, 1985

Birthplace: Las Vegas, Nevada

Hometown: Denver, North Carolina

Children: 2

AWARDS

NASCAR Cup Series Champion: 2015, 2019

NASCAR Cup Series Regular Season Champion: 2018, 2019

NASCAR Xfinity Series Champion: 2009

NASCAR Xfinity Series Rookie of the Year: 2004

NASCAR national series wins record holder: 231

GLOSSARY

box stock A class of racing cars resembling go-karts for young drivers.

debut First time to perform in public.

generation A time period when people of about the same age live.

Legends Race cars that look like 1930s and 1940s American cars but are ⅝-scale.

motivate To create interest or give a reason to do something.

short track Racetracks that are less than a mile.

24/7 Championship A World Wrestling Entertainment (WWE) title that could be won by anyone at any time as long as a WWE referee was present.

READ MORE

Abdo, Kenny. **Kyle Busch.** Minneapolis, MN: Abdo Publishing, 2022.

Koestler-Grack, Rachel A. **Stock Cars.** Mankato, MN: Amicus, 2023.

ON THE WEB

Kyle Busch
https://kylebusch.com/

Kyle Busch facts for kids
https://kids.kiddle.co/Kyle_Busch

NASCAR KIDS
https://www.nascarkids.com/

INDEX

About the Author

Mary Bleckwehl is a children's author who loves cookie dough and talking to kids. She is happiest when she is biking and exploring new places. Mary lives in Minnesota with her husband and monster dog. Check out her books at marybleckwehl.com.